God talks with me about Comfort

Published by iCharacter Ltd. (Ireland)
www.iCharacter.org
By Agnes and Salem de Bezenac
Illustrated by Agnes de Bezenac
Colored by Noviyanti W.
Copyright 2016. All rights reserved.
All Bible verses adapted from the KJV.

Anita always looked forward to those special moments when Mom and Dad would come to tuck her into bed.

Mom and Dad always listened intently as Anita talked about her new friends at school and about the games she played at recess.

Anita prayed, "Now I lay me down to sleep, I pray the Lord my soul to keep..."

Anita then bounced out of bed to get her favorite Bible book. "I'll pick a verse for tonight," she said.

It was the same one that she had picked last night and the night before that, and the night before that, too. Dad and Mom had lost count of how many times they read the same verse to her.

But in her gentle voice
Mom read again:

"I lie down in peace and sleep because You, Lord, keep me safe."
(Psalms 4:8)

As soon as they had finished reading, Anita asked excitedly, "Daddy, will you please sing me one of your songs?"

Dad cleared his throat and began to sing while Mom and Anita swayed gracefully to the music.

When the song was done, Mom and Dad kissed Anita good night. Then —

Click! Click!

— went the lights.

After her parents had left
the room, Anita heard a loud,
squeaking noise.

"What was that?" she wondered aloud.

"Sweetheart, it's only the door creaking,"
Mother reassured her from down the hall.

Anita pulled the music player from under
her pillow and put on a song to listen to.
When I am afraid, I put my trust in You...

A little while later, a creepy shadow
appeared on her bedroom wall.

It's a ghost! she thought to herself
as she hid under the covers.

"Jesus, I don't like being alone
in the dark. I'm afraid."

Soon, she heard another faint sound:

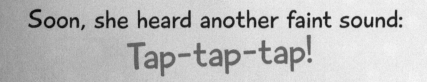

Tap-tap-tap!

Anita turned on her bedside lamp.
She felt just a little braver in the light.

Reaching for her Bible, she read
another favorite verse, "God is our
protection and our strength. He always
helps in times of trouble."

Tap-tap-tap! —came the noise again!

"Dear God, I'm still scared!
Please help me to be brave."

Anita finally built up her courage and slipped
out of bed. As she crept toward the shadows
that danced on her wall, she repeated the
verse, "Jesus, I will not be afraid because
You are right here with me."

Anita shut her eyes tightly hoping that the shadows would go away, but when she opened them again they were still on her wall.

This isn't a dream, she thought to herself.

Turning to the window, she realized
that the scary shapes on her wall were
just the shadows of tree branches,
moving in the moonlight.

Laughing to
herself, she
thought, *Why
was I scared
over that?
That's silly
of me.*

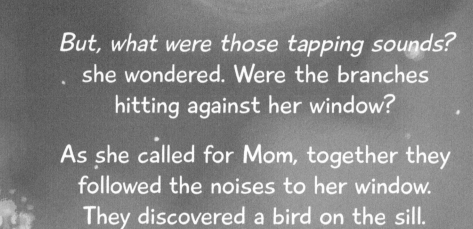

But, what were those tapping sounds? she wondered. Were the branches hitting against her window?

As she called for Mom, together they followed the noises to her window. They discovered a bird on the sill.

"Oh, you poor thing! It looks like you fell out of your nest!" Anita said.

Spotting a nest on a nearby branch, she placed the little bird back in it's home.

"Don't worry, little birdie," Anita said. "Everything will be all right."

A Bible verse suddenly came to Anita's mind: "Not even one sparrow can fall to the ground without your Father knowing it."

*If God watches over a tiny little bird, then I'm sure
He is watching over me, too,* she thought. "Thank You for
caring for all of Your little creatures, including me!"

Anita jumped back into her cozy bed
and snuggled under her warm blanket.

Her eyes fell on the cover of her Bible.
*I love that picture. It makes me feel
like I am one of those kids in*
Jesus's arms, she thought.

Suddenly she heard another sound— a faint Buzz! Buzz!

It wasn't a bird and it wasn't the swaying branches of the tree.

She quietly tiptoed towards the bathroom and peeked in.
"Nope, it's not coming from here," she said. So, she listened again.

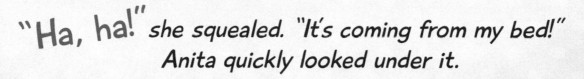

"Ha, ha!" she squealed. "It's coming from my bed!"
Anita quickly looked under it.

"There's nothing here!" she exclaimed. Then she looked
under the covers. "Nothing here, either!"

Then she lifted her pillow.

"Oh. It's just my music player! The battery must
have run low," she laughed as she turned it off.

She got back into bed. Now there was nothing
left to be afraid of. "Dear God," she prayed.
"Thank You for taking such good care of me."

"I have nothing to fear because You watch over me. Just like I helped that little bird, I know that You care for me too. Like it says in Your Word, 'The Lord Who watches over you will not slumber nor sleep.'"

Then Anita dozed off into dreamland where she dreamt of a little bird, all cozy and warm, sleeping in its nest.

Something to read

You can find the Bible verses by following the references.

- "I lie down in peace and sleep because You, Lord, keep me safe" (Psalms 4:8)

- "When I am afraid, I put my trust in You." (Psalms 56:3)

- "God is our protection and our strength. He always helps in times of trouble." (Psalms 46:1)

- "I will not be afraid, for You are close beside me." (Psalms 118:6)

- "Not even one sparrow can fall to the ground without your Father knowing it." (Matthew 10:29)

- What are some things that make you feel scared when you are alone?

- What do you usually do when you feel afraid? Sometimes it's good just to call Mommy, Daddy or someone who is taking care of you. When is it good to call them if you are afraid?

- What helped Anita not to be afraid?

Something to do

You will need:

- A glass
- A tray
- Stones

● Here's a simple little object lesson to help your children understand what courage means.

● Fill the glass with water as you explain how water, like fear, can be splashed around and make things worse. Take turns giving examples of courage depending on the particular fear. For example, if there is a fear of the dark, discuss what to do: pray, remember parents are nearby, remember prayers said, and so on.

● For each example of courage, drop a stone in the glass. The more the glass fills with rocks of courage the more fear spills out and flows away.

Lightning Source UK Ltd.
Milton Keynes UK
UKOW07f1346060417
298510UK00004B/10/P